DEDICATION

To all the parents who value the Greek language enough to send their children to Greek school, and to all those Greek-Australian children who persevere and attend Greek school. It may be tough at times but the rewards are many.

Published by HELLENIC THEOREM PUBLISHERS.

© Text and music copyright Eleni Elefterias-Kostakidis.

Eleni Elefterias
PO Box 513 Ashfield NSW 2131
elenielefterias.com.au
eleni@elenielefterias.com.au
hellenictheorem@gmail.com

First published 2022 by Grammatakia.com
New edition published 2023 by Hellenic Theorem Publishers.

The moral right of author and illustrator has been asserted.

Layout by Oliver Milgate

All rights reserved. No part of this publication may be reproduced, stored in a retrieval system, or transmitted in any form or in any means - by electronic, mechanical, photocopying, recording or otherwise - without prior written permission.

ISBN: 978-0-6489128-5-9 (Paperback)

Αρκάδι 10-6-62

Αγαπητά μου εγγόνια Μένιο, Αντωνία
μου, Λούλα. Είδα μωρέ την εικόνα σας βγαλμένη
και όταν σας εξιδώ εις την φωτογραφία
πάνου, τα μάτια μου δακρίζουνε και όσες σας
βγάλανε εις εις φωτογραφίες και ογοί
έργονται σε οπτικά γιατί μία Μίταλα Βασιλι-
κούλα Θείου και εμείς αγαπητά εγγόνια.
Άκουσε, έχει να συναντώ σων μεγάλα
εγγονικά και άλλα αγαπημένα μου εγγόνια να
ξέρετε και τα εγγλέζικα μιας και η
γιαγιά σου με την αννούλα μου άρμοζα
ιδού με συμπλέατε όταν σας βγούνε να
εγγλέζικα, όμοι με συναντώ και οι δασκάλες σα
και όλοι οι βιαζάδες με συναντάνε για άπα
μωρέ άρχισε να μάθεις εντα μωρέ τα
εγγρίζετε και εγγλέζικα. Η γράψετε εις
το γράμμα σας, ότι έχε εδώ όσα ο ωεβίς
μου, εγγόνικα αλλά φυσικός ούτε γράμο δε ειδι
και το μωρόλι μου ήταν ιδώ αγαπητό και
σας ευχάρι όταν έρθετε εις την Ελλάδα
να ε μάθετε και σας όσοι ένα τέτοιο.
αυξιθέ αρά ότι εν γράφω, έπαι, Σάββατο
και εώηγαμε εις τη Συγνακά και έβραδιαμε

ΘΕΛΩ ΝΑ ΜΑΘΩ ΕΛΛΗΝΙΚΑ

I WANT TO LEARN GREEK

A SONG BY ELENI ELEFTERIAS

Scan the QR Code to access video and audio.
---------------->

Performed by Nick Antonoglou and Marina Thiveos and the Thelo Na Matho Ellinika Choir and Band

Θέλω να μάθω ελληνικά

THE-lo   na   MA-tho   e-lli-ni-KA

να μιλώ με τη γιαγιά,

na   mi-LO   me   ti   yia-YIA

(I want to learn greek
to speak with grandma,)

τον ξάδελφό μου
ton KSA-thel-FO moo

τον Μηνά,
ton Mi-NA

(my cousin Mina)

τον Θείο Γιώργο

ton   THI-o   YIO-rgho

τον μπεκρή

ton   be-KRI

(my Uncle George the drunk)

11

κι όλο το σόι
ki   O-lo   to   SO-i

στην Κομοτηνή
stin   ko-mo-ti-NI

(and all the family in Komotini)

και μαθαίναμε πότε
kai ma-THE-na-me PO-te

καλά πότε στραβά,
ka-LA PO-te stra-VA

(and we learned sometimes
Well and sometimes not)

Τι θα πουν τα λόγια του
Ti tha poun ta LO-yia tou

Πάτερ ημών, εξήγηση
PA-ter im-ON e-KSI-yi-si

καμία στο σχολείο.
ka-MI-a sto skho-LI-o

(What do the words of the Lord's prayer mean, no explanation at school.)

Τι σημαίνει ο Ύμνος;
ti si-ME-ni o IM-nos

Ποιος είναι ο Σολωμός;
Pios I-ne o So-lo-MOS

(What is the meaning of the Hymn?
Who is Solomos?)

Τι έγινε την εικοστή
ti   E-yi-ne   tin   i-kos-TI

πρώτη Απριλίου;
PRO-ti   a-pri-LI-ou

(What happened on the 21st of April?)

22

Έλα, Έλλη, έλα.
E-lla   E-lli   E-lla

(Come, Elli, come.)

Έλα, Μίμη, πάρε.
E-lla   MI-mi   PA-re

Πάρε, Άννα, μήλο.
PA-re   A-nna   MI-lo

(Come, Mimi, take one.)
(Take an apple, Anna.)

Μήλο μου, μαχαίρι.
MI-lo   moo   ma-HE-ri

Έλα, Έλλη, έλα.
E-lla   E-lli   E-lla

(My apple, a knife.)
(Come Elli come.)

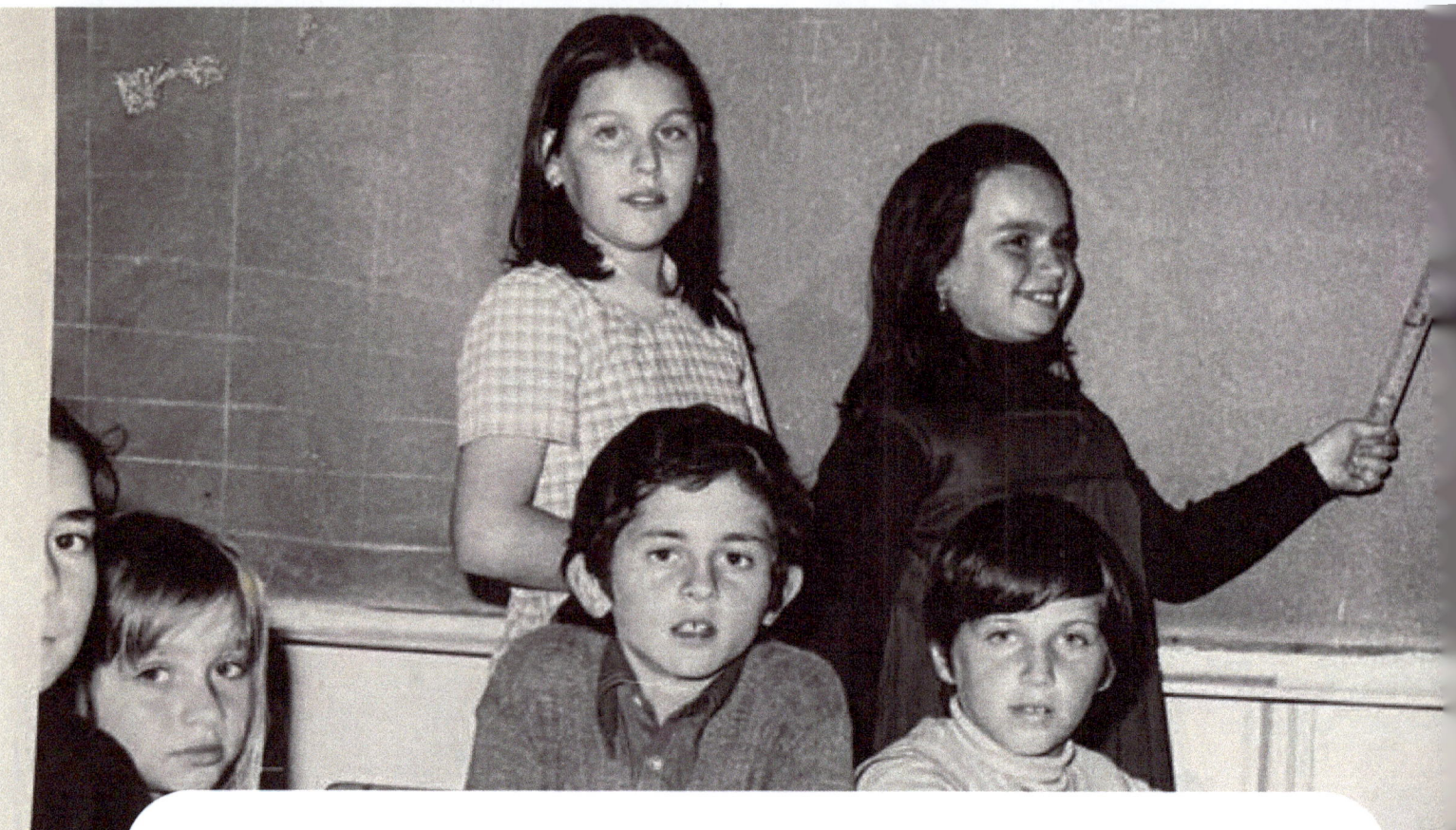

Θέλω να μάθω ελληνικά
THE-lo na MA-tho e-lli-ni-KA

να γράφω γράμματα πολλά,
na GHRA-fo GHRA-ma-ta po-LLA

(I want to learn Greek to write lots of letters.)

τραγούδια

tra-GHOU-thia

καλαματιανά,

ka-la-ma-ti-a-NA

(Songs, Kalamatiana dances)

Να χορέψω ζεϊμπεκιά,
Na ho-RE-pso zei-be-KIA

Με τον παππού μου
me ton pa-POU moo

άλλη μια φορά.

A-lli   mia   fo-RA

(To dance a zembekiko,
with my grandad one more time.)

Ελληνικό χορό τα
E-lli-ni-KO   ho-RO   ta

Σαββατόβραδα, με
Sa-va-TO-vra-tha   me

σουβλάκια σε πιάτα
sou-VLA-ki-a   se   PIA-ta

πλαστικά,
pla-sti-KA

(Greek dances on Saturday nights, with souvlaki on plastic plates,)

Εθνικές γιορτές και
Eth-ni-KES yi-or-TES ke

παρέλαση, αμαλίες και
Pa-RE-la-si a-ma-LI-es ke

Τσολιάδες στη σειρά.
Tso-LIA-thes sti si-RA

(National days and parades, amalias and tsoliades in a row.)

Βαπτίσια και κεριά
Vap-TI-si-a ke ke-RIA

κλαίγαν τα μωρά, με
KLE-ghan   ta   mo-RA   me

τους σταυρούς
tous   stav-ROUS

δεμένους στα λαιμά,
the-ME-nous   sta   le-MA

(Baptisms and candles, babies crying,
with crosses tied to their necks,)

προέδρους και παπάδες
pro-E-throus   ke   pa-PA-thes

και καλαματιανά,
ke ka-la-ma-tia-NA

(Presidents, priests, Kalamatiana dances,)

Αυτά Θυμάμαι μα
Af-TA   thi-MA-me   ma

εξήγηση καμιά.
e-KSI-yi-si   ka-MIA

(That's what I remember
but never an explanation)

Έλα, Έλλη, έλα.
E-lla   E-lli   E-lla

(Come, Elli, come.)

Έλα, Μίμη, πάρε.
E-lla MI-mi PA-re

Πάρε, Άννα, μήλο.
PA-re A-nna MI-lo

(Come, Mimi, take one,)
(Take an apple, Anna.)

Μήλο μου, μαχαίρι.
MI-lo   moo   ma-KHE-ri

(My apple, a knife.)

Ἔλα, Ἔλλη, ἔλα.
E-lla   E-lli   E-lla

(Come, Elli, come.)

Άλφα, βήτα, γάμμα, δέλτα,
AL-fa,   VI-ta,   GHA-mma, THEL-ta,

έψιλον, ζήτα, ήτα, Θήτα,
E-psi-lon,   ZI-ta   I-ta,   THI-ta,

ιώτα, κάππα, λάμδα, μι,
YO-ta,   KA-ppa   LAM-tha   mi

(alpha, bita, gamma, thelta, epsilon,
zita, ita, thita, yiota, kappa, lamda, mi,)

νι, ξι, όμικρον, πι, ρο,
ni ksi O-mi-kron pi ro

σίγμα, ταυ, ύψιλον, φι,
SI-ghma taf I-psi-lon fi

χι, ψι, ωμέγα.
khi psi o-ME-gha

(ni, xi, omicron, pi, ro, sigma, tau,
ipsilon, fi, chi, psi, omega.)

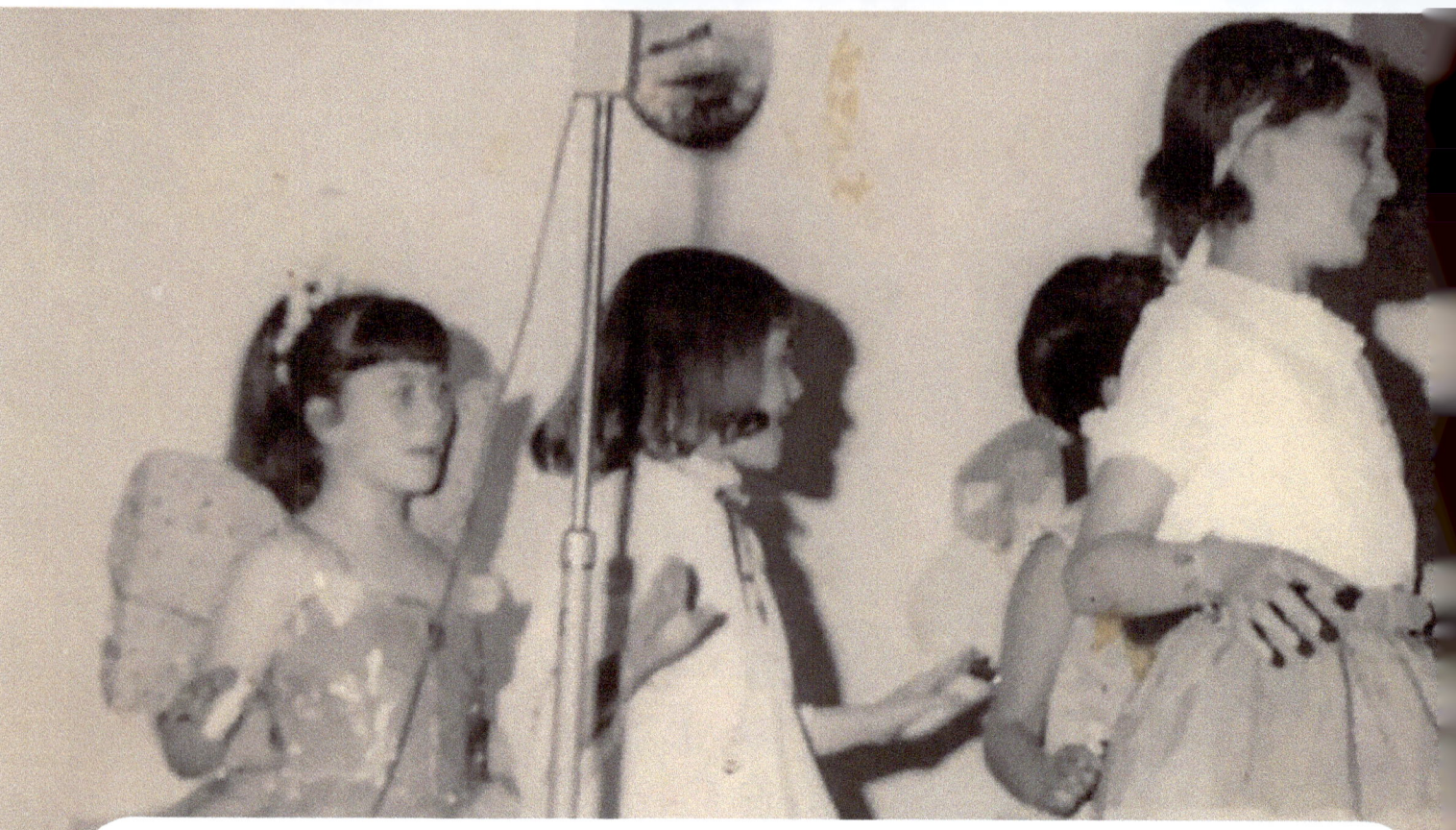

Έλα, Έλλη, έλα. Έλα, Μίμη, πάρε.
E-lla　　E-lli　　E-lla　　E-lla　　MI-mi　　PA-re

Πάρε, Άννα, μήλο.
PA-re　　A-nna　　MI-lo

(Come, Elli, come. Come, Mimi, take.
Take an apple, Anna.)

Όλα τα ελληνικά,
O-la ta e-lli-ni-KA

πολύ τα αγαπώ,
Po-LI ta a-gha-PO

(Everything Greek, I love a lot,)

Μα πιο πολύ απ'όλα
ma pio po-LI ap'-O-lla

(But more than anything)

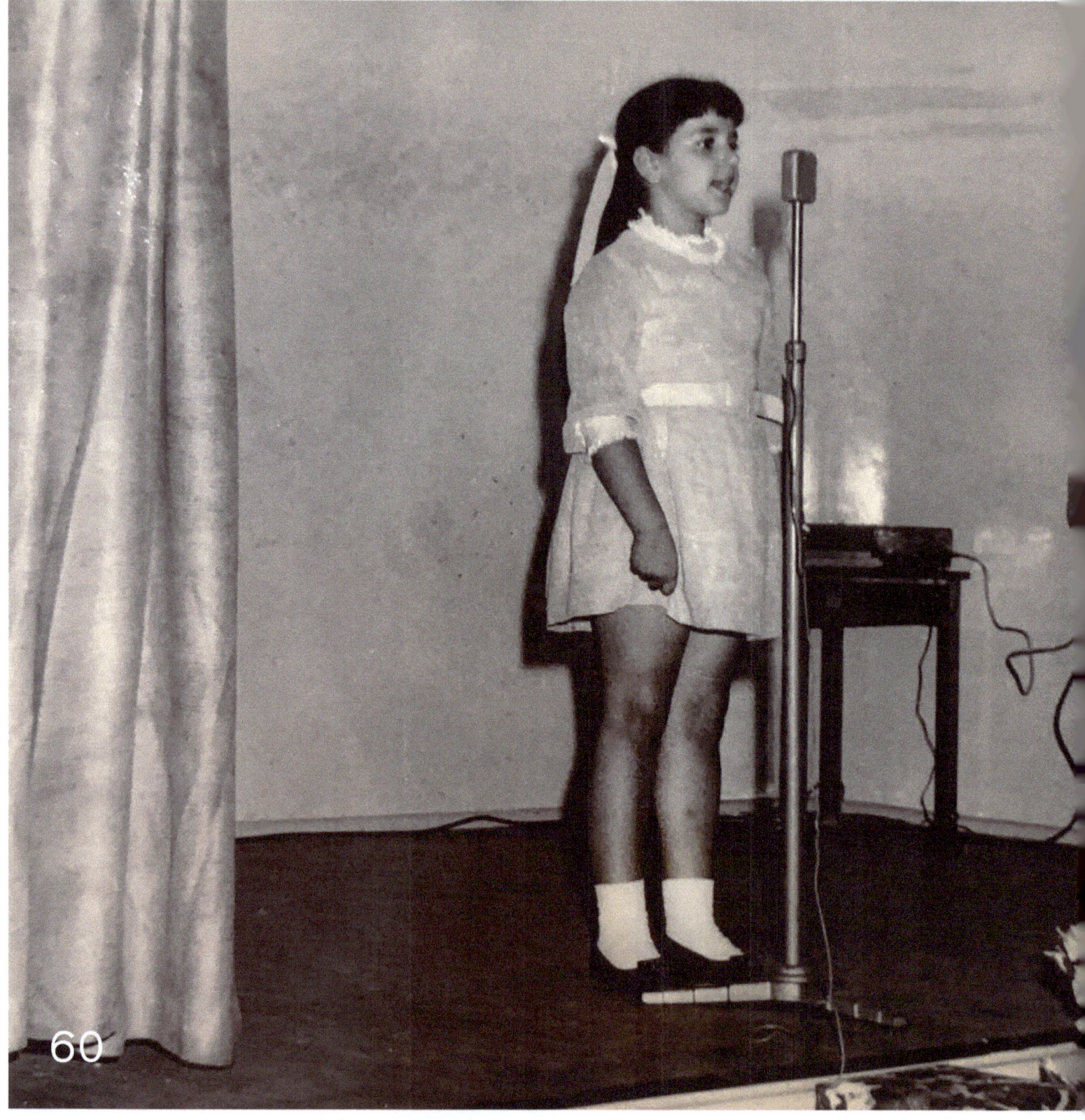

Θέλω να μάθω ελληνικά
THE-lo   na   MA-tho   e-lli-ni-KA

να μιλώ με τη γιαγιά!
Na   mi-LO   me   ti   yia-YIA

(I want to learn Greek to
speak with my grandma!)

Θέλω να μάθω ελληνικά

THE-lo na MA-tho e-lli-ni-KA

(I want to learn Greek)

να μιλώ με τη γιαγιά!
Na mi-LO me ti yia-YIA

(to speak with my grandma!)

CREDITS

Music and lyrics by Eleni Elefterias. Music and choir arrangement by Felicia Harris. Sound engineer Daniel Natoli at A Sharp Studios. Musical accompaniment by Paul Hofstetter (guitar), Zisis Koustoulis (percussion), Daniel Natoli (Electric Guitar and Bass). Rap performed by Nicholas Antonoglou and lead vocals by Marina Thiveos. The THELO NA MATHO ELLINIKA CHOIR led by Felicia Harris, with Eleni Elefterias, Christine Gazepis-Stavropoulos, Joanne Mayson, Mersina Papantoniou, Persefoni Sue Thliveris and Eva Tzodouris.

Child singers: Lukas Moustakis, Anna Eleftheriou and Nefeli Eleftheriou.

Video: Directed and mastered by Yannis Nikolakopoulos.

Actors: Nicholas Antonoglou, Marina Thiveos, Zisis Koustoulis, Eleni Elefterias, Felicia Harris, Jason Antonoglou, Alekos Kaltsas, Kaliope Diamantis, Alexandra Pennell, Lukas Moustakis, Sam Pappas, Anna and Nefeli Eleftheriou, Shirley Peshos. Makeup: Petros Hovaghimian. Roadies and Helpers: Christos Kyvetos, Alex Missiris, Sue Thliveris and Niki Eleftheriou.

PICTURE INDEX

Cover: Greek Afternoon School, 1948, Evagelismos School, Melbourne

Page 2 Letter from Theodoroula Prineas to her son Peter Prineas, Jandowae Qld, 10th June, 1962, supplied by Emmanuel Prineas

Page 5 All Saints Church Belmore Greek Afternoon School with Mrs Angela Gemenis on the piano, Teacher: Mary Georgeson c.1970's, supplied by Cathy Defteros

Page 6 Earlwood Greek Independent Afternoon School, c. 1985, supplied by Sofia Lucas (pictured).

Page 9 Marrickville PS After School Greek Class, 1974, supplied by Penny Thliveris (pictured)

Page 10 Camdenville Public School Greek Afternoon School, 1979, supplied by Kathy Kouvas (pictured).

Pages 12-13 Earlwood Independent school c 1986-87, supplied by Sofia Lucas.

Pages 14-15 All Saints Belmore Archdiocese Greek School, Teacher: Vasiliki Fotiadis, Students: Cathy Defteros, Christine Kotsouris, Betty Pappas, Steven Vasil c,1970's supplied by Cathy Defteros

Page 17 Father Izekiel (later Bishop in Melboune), All Saints Belmore Archdiocese Greek School, c.1975, supplied by Cathy Defteros.

Page 18, Persa Mousmoutis, Saint Sofia Greek Orthodox Community of NSW School Paddington, Teacher was Mrs Fofi Alexiadou c.1973, Supplied by Persa Sue Thliveris

Page 19 Dionysion Solomos National Poet of Greece who wrote the poem Ode to Freedom, the Greek National Anthem.

Page 20 Junta historical poster (April 1967-74) shown in many Greek schools of that era.

Page 21 Dimitra Tzodouris, Canterbury Greek School, 1994, supplied by Eva Tzodouris.

Pages 22-23 Taken from the original Arlfavitario book by I.K.Gianelis, originally published by Kalokathis, depicting Elli, Lola, Anna and Mimi.

Page 25 Pamela Lucas, Earlwood Independent Greek Afternoon School, c. 1985, supplied by Sofia Lucas.

Page 26-27 Greek Orthodox Community of NSW Greek School, c.1970's, from the archives of the GOC, Sydney.

Page 28 Earlwood Independent Greek School c.1983, supplied by Sofia Lucas (pictured)

Page 31-32 Pamela Lucas Earlwood Independent Greek School, c.1983-84, supplied by Sofia Lucas (also pictured).
Page 32 Greek Orthodox Community of NSW Greek School celebration, c. 1970's, from the Archives of the GOC, Sydney.
Pages 34-35 Earlwood Independent Greek School march, c.1980's, supplied by Sofia Lucas.
Page 36 Greek Church 28th October OXI day celebration, from the Archives of the GOC NSW.
Page 38-39 Earlwood Independent Greek School, c.1980's, supplied by Sofia Lucas (pictured)
Page 41, Earlwood Independent School c. 1980's, supplied by Sofia Lucas (pictured).
Page 42, Belmore All Saints Greek Archdiocese Afternoon School, c.1963, supplied by Alexandra Missiris (pictured).
Page 45 North Strathfield Greek School, c.1974, supplied by Kathy Kokori (pictured)
Page 47 Camdenville PS Greek Afternoon School, 1976, supplied by Kathy Kouvas (pictured).
Page 48 Bourke St Greek Afternoon School, teacher Kyria Froso c. Late 1960's-early 1970's, supplied by Petros Kagelaris.
Page 53 Earlwood Independent Greek School march, c.1980's, supplied by Sofia Lucas.
Page 54-55 Earlwood Independent Greek School march, c.1980's, supplied by Sofia Lucas.
Page 56 Persa Mousmoutis, Greek Orthodox Community of NSW, St Sophia Greek School Paddington, Teacher was Kyria Alexiadou, c.early 1970's, supplied by Persa Sue Thliveris.
Pages 58-59 Persa Mousmoutis, Greek Orthodox Community of NSW, St Sophia Greek School Paddington, early 1970's, supplied by Persa Sue Thliveris.
Pages 60-61 The new generation, Aristotelis Greek Language Education Afternoon School, North Strathfield PS, December 2021
Page 62 Camdenville PS Greek Afternoon School, 1976, supplied by Kathy Kouvas (pictured).
Page 63 Eleftheria and Jacinta Kostakidis (Melissakia Greek Program, St Peters), granddaughters of the author, 2022. Photo Tammy Siriak
Page 65 The performers of the music recording and some of those who appeared in the video as well. c. 2017-2018
Front cover: Melbourne Greek Evagelismos Church 1948
Back Cover: Video Performers

GREEKLISH GUIDE

A α	άλφα	Alpha	fAther
B β	βήτα	Vita	Vital
Γ γ	γάμμα	GHamma (Y as in yellow, YI as in year or GH, between game + yard)	Yes
Δ δ	δέλτα	THelta (Hard th)	Then
E ε	έψιλον	Epsilon	Egg
Z ζ	ζήτα	Zita	Zebra
H η	ήτα	Ita	India, Era
Θ θ	θήτα	THita (Soft th)	THrone
I ι	ιώτα	Iota	India, Era
K κ	κάππα	Kappa	Kitchen
Λ λ	λάμδα	Lamtha	Lamb
M μ	μι	Mi	Mother

Ν ν	νι	Ni	Nice
Ξ ξ	ξι	KSi (Like x)	taXi
Ο ο	όμικρον	Omicron	hOt
Π π	πι	Pi	Peanut
Ρ ρ	ρω	Ro (rolled on the front of the tongue)	Rock
Σ σ ς	σίγμα	Sigma	Sand
Τ τ	ταύ	Tuf	Tennis
Υ υ	ύψιλον	Ipsilon	India
Φ φ	φι	Fi	Fine
Χ χ	χι	Hi	Hair, How
Ψ ψ	ψι	PSi	liPS
Ω ω	ωμέγα	Omegha	hOt

Note to parents and teachers

The book is meant to be read phonetically. For free audio examples, pronunciation guides and educational materials go to eleni@elenielefterias.com.au or YouTube & Tiktok: #elenielefterias.

ACKNOWLEDGEMENTS

Thank you to all the performers, musicians and actors who took part in this project. To the Greek Orthodox Community of NSW for permission to use the photos, and all those who provided the pictures and whose names appear in the book. To Felicia Harris for her ongoing support in arranging and organising the choir and musicians. To Anna Iouannidou of the Greek Orthodox Community of NSW Archive Centre. To photographer Effie Alexakis for help with the choice of photos and Dr Alfred Vincent for his advice and help with final editing. To the bilingualbookshop.com.au for supporting local authors. To project sponsors Felicia Harris and Vasilis Gonopoulos & Elfa Moraitakis of the Aristotelis Greek Language school, and also La Boîte Performance Space and Patreon Sponsors: Jill-Catherine Papadopoulos, Persefoni Sue Thliveris, Eleni Kokkinos and Jean Tsembis. Special thanks to Yannis

Eleni Elefterias is an academic and teacher of Modern Greek who enjoys composing songs, lyrics and stories for children. This book is suitable for the teaching of Modern Greek on the topics of Identity, Education, Family and Migration to students of all ages.